GO FOR IT! ™

SOFTBALL

FOR BOYS AND GIRLS

START RIGHT AND PLAY WELL

D1312573

by Bill Gutman
with Illustrations
by Ben Brown

SAUNDERS
BOOK COMPANY

GREY CASTLE PRESS

Published by arrangement with Grey Castle Press, Lakeville, Ct.

Copyright © 1990 by Grey Castle Press.
Saunders Book Company
Canadian Library Edition

The *GO FOR IT* Sports Series is a trademark of Grey Castle Press.

Printed in the USA

The Library of Congress Cataloging in Publication Data

Gutman, Bill.
    Softball : start right and play well / by Bill Gutman ; with illustrations by Ben Brown.
      p.   cm. — (Go for it!)
   Summary: Describes the history and current teams, leagues, and championships of softball and provides instruction on how to play the game.
   ISBN 0-942545-91-5 (lib. bdg.)
   1. Softball—Juvenile literature. [1. Softball.] I. Brown, Ben, 1921–   Ill. II. Title. III. Series: Gutman, Bill. Go for it!
GV867.5.G89   1990
796.357'8—dc20

89-7608
CIP
AC

Photo credits: Joan E. Chandler, page 8, left and right; The National Baseball Hall of Fame and Museum, Inc.

Special thanks to: Bill Zmudosky, varsity softball coach, Dover Junior/Senior High School, Dover Plains, N.Y.

Picture research: Omni Photo Communications, Inc.

Saunders Book Company
Canadian Library Edition
ISBN 1-895058-06-6

ABOUT THE AUTHOR

Bill Gutman is the author of over 70 books for children and young adults. The majority of his titles have dealt with sports, in both fiction and non-fiction, including "how-to" books. His name is well-known to librarians who make it their business to be informed about books of special interest to boys and reluctant readers. He lives in Poughquag, New York.

ABOUT THE ILLUSTRATOR

Ben Brown's experience ranges from cartoonist to gallery painter. He is a graduate of the High School of Music & Art in New York City and the University of Iowa Art School. He has been a member of the National Academy of Design and the Art Students' League. He has illustrated government training manuals for the disadvantaged (using sports as themes), and his animation work for the American Bible Society won two blue ribbons from the American Film Festival. He lives in Great Barrington, Massachusetts.

In order to keep the instructions in this book as simple as possible, the author has chosen in most cases to use "he" to signify both boys and girls.

A BRIEF HISTORY

Softball is an American game. Oddly enough, two different men seem to have invented it about eight years apart. The first was George Hancock, a reporter and a member of the Farragut Boat Club in Chicago. In 1887, Hancock was looking for a game like baseball, which was still a young sport, that could be played indoors.

Hancock's first ball was an old boxing glove. He wrapped some string around it to make it round and threw it underhand to another man who tried to hit it with an old broomstick.

Eight years later, in 1895, a fireman in Minnesota, Lewis Rober, did almost the exact same thing. He wanted a game like baseball that he and his fireman friends would be able to play indoors. Since evidence shows that Rober did not know about Hancock's game, both men are credited with inventing softball.

The game grew slowly, began to spread and eventually moved outdoors. It wasn't long before some type of softball was being played in backyards, on playgrounds or at picnics. It was played anywhere people got together to have some fun.

There were different forms of the game then, and different rules. It was even called by different names, like ''big ball,'' ''mush ball'' and ''playground ball.'' Fields were of various sizes. The balls were made of different materials and no two were the same size. Even the rules were different. While it was a fun game, it wasn't really an organized sport.

Then, in the early 1930s, the game began growing even faster. In 1933, the American Softball Association was founded. A committee was formed to makes standard rules for everyone to use. The game was finally given one name—softball. Since that time, the game has grown by leaps and bounds and has spread to many different countries.

The first national tournament between Industrial League teams was held in Chicago in 1933. The first worldwide tournament for women was held in Melbourne, Australia, in 1965. A year later, the men played a worldwide tournament for the first time. The sport has continued to spread and grow ever since.

Because the game was first played indoors on a smaller field, overhand pitching was sometimes too fast. Therefore, the rules were changed to make the pitcher throw underhand. This helped for a while. Pretty soon there were pitchers who could throw nearly as fast as overhand baseball pitchers.

Some of them could whip the softball in at nearly 100 miles an hour. The pitchers, both men and women, became the most famous softball players. There was a pitcher named Clarence ''Buck'' Miller who pitched nearly 100 no-hit games during his career. A woman named Betty Grayson held a record of 115 straight scoreless innings. She was so fast that her nickname was ''Bullet Betty.''

Two other pitchers made big names for themselves in softball. Eddie Feigner was so good that he only played with three other men in the field behind him. Feigner called his team ''The King and his Court'' and traveled around the country playing nine-man teams. He rarely lost a game.

Feigner might have been the best all-around softball pitcher ever. Not only would he throw regulation pitches, but he could also pitch between his legs, behind his back, from second base and while blindfolded. The result was almost always the same; another strikeout for the King.

Eddie Feigner in action. He was one of the greatest softball pitchers ever, as well as one of the few to become well-known. Touring the United States with his four-man team, known as "The King and His Court," Feigner displayed his great pitching skills to fans.

While Eddie Feigner used his skills to barnstorm with his four-man team, Joan Joyce used hers to pitch in organized softball. She pitched for the Raybestos Brakettes, a team from Waterbury, Connecticut. With Joan on the mound, the Brakettes were national champions a number of times.

How good was Joan Joyce? Well, in the 1973 Women's National Championships, she pitched all nine of her team's games. She lost one, 1–0, on an unearned run, the result of an error. In the other eight games, she pitched eight shutouts. She pitched two no-hitters, three one-hitters and four two-hitters. In nine games, she walked just one batter and struck out 134. When Joan Joyce retired from competitive softball, she became a professional golfer.

There are others who have worked as hard as Joyce or Feigner to become skilled at the sport. These are the great ones, the select few. But there are also millions of others, boys and girls, young and old, enjoying the sport that was invented as an indoor substitute for baseball. It is out on its own now and still growing.

Though many consider her to be the greatest woman softball pitcher of all time, Joan Joyce was an all-around player who could also swing the bat very well. As a pitcher, she was so good that even professional baseball players had trouble hitting her softball offerings during exhibition games.

ORGANIZED SOFTBALL

Softball today is the most popular team sport in America. It is part of nearly every school's sports program, either in physical education classes or on a competitive level. Young people begin playing in elementary school and can continue right through high school. Most cities and towns have their own softball leagues. Kids can play, as well as old timers. In that sense, softball is a sport for everyone.

In fact, one reason that softball has spread to many other countries has been the United States' armed forces. Men and women in the Army and Navy have played the game everywhere they've been. In recent years, members of the Peace Corps have also taken the sport to different foreign lands.

Even though there are national tournaments and a few professional players, softball has remained largely an amateur sport. Most people play for fun and exercise, and that makes the sport very special.

The American Softball Association, also called the Amateur Softball Association (ASA), is still the governing body. There is also an International Softball Association, founded in 1952, which helps to organize the sport in more than 40 countries.

For young players 12 and under, ASA tournaments go only to the state level. But for 13 to 15 year olds, and 16 to 18 year olds, tournaments are held on both the regional and national levels.

These are for both boys and girls and include "slow" and "fast" pitch softball. There are also organized ASA tournaments for adults.

Any junior or amateur team can register with the ASA and become eligible to enter one of their tournaments. Information on tournaments, as well as a free rule book, is available from the ASA. Anyone interested can write to the ASA at 2801 N.E. 50th Street, P.O. Box 11437, Oklahoma City, Oklahoma 73111.

Softball has never stopped growing. Today there are all kinds of leagues, even ones for fathers and sons and mothers and daughters. There are Boy Scout and Girl Scouts leagues and special leagues for senior citizens. Softball is simply everywhere. It's fun to play and easy to learn. It's really a game that everyone should know.

The Game Of Softball

Baseball and softball are alike in many ways. Both sports involve pitching and hitting. They each use three bases and a home plate. In each game, the infield portion of the field is called a diamond, and the fielding positions are very similar. Of course, the object of the game is the same—to score runs by circling the bases and crossing home plate safely.

As in baseball, the team at bat hits until three outs are made. Then the teams switch, and the fielding team comes in to hit. Base hits and outs are made the same ways as in baseball. Though he throws underhand, the pitcher starts by throwing the ball toward the catcher, with the batter waiting to hit it.

The hitters come up one by one. There are nine hitters in "fast pitch" softball, but in the "slow pitch" game there are 10. The basic batting order is also similar to baseball. Batters do not have to swing at each pitch. There is an umpire to call strikes and balls.

Home plate is 17 inches wide. After three strikes, the batter is out. After four balls, he takes first base on a walk.

As in baseball, the batter tries to hit the ball between or over the fielders. If a batter reaches first base, he has hit a single. If he reaches second, he has doubled. If he gets to third on a safe hit, he has tripled. And if he can circle all the bases, then he has a home run. But it is usually a combination of hits that produces a team's runs.

Outs can be made on strikes or by a fielder catching a ball hit in the air. A batter is also out if the player fielding the ball throws it to first base before the batter gets there. Of course, the first baseman must have his foot on the bag.

While all these basics are the same as baseball, there are some things in softball that are different. The underhand pitching has already been mentioned. There are also two kinds of softball pitching. Fast pitch means the pitcher can throw as hard as he or she can. Besides throwing hard, the top pitchers can throw curves, change-ups, drops and rises. Pitching is the most important part of fast pitch softball.

The slow pitch game is very different. It was meant more for fun. In slow pitch, the object is to let everyone hit and to allow the fielders to use their skills. The pitcher can only throw the ball at a moderate speed. The ball must also have an arc of between three and 10 feet.

In recent years, lob, or arc, ball has also become popular. In this version of softball, the ball is pitched with an even higher arc, up to 12 feet. Again, the pitcher's only real skill is to get the ball over the plate. Lob ball is also made for the hitter, but it takes practice to time a ball floating down from such a high arc.

In the old days, fast pitch was the most popular form of softball, but today, about 75 percent of all softball in the United States is the slow pitch type.

Besides the pitching, there are a couple of other differences between slow and fast pitch softball. Fast pitch has nine players, just like baseball, but slow pitch has 10. The extra player is usually a short fielder. Because there is more hitting in slow pitch, the extra fielder helps the defense keep the score down.

There is no bunting or base stealing in slow pitch softball. Both are allowed in fast pitch, however. But base runners in fast pitch cannot lead off a base the way they can in baseball. They must keep at least one foot on the base until the the ball leaves the pitcher's hand. In slow pitch, a base runner cannot leave the bag until the ball is hit.

Another difference between baseball and softball is the length of the game. Baseball games at the college and professional levels are nine innings long. Softball games are only seven innings long at all levels.

The Field And Equipment

The softball field is smaller than the baseball field. In the adult game, the bases are 60 feet apart, compared to 90 feet apart in baseball. The softball pitching rubber is 46 feet from home plate, instead of 60. Outfield fences can vary, but no fence can be less than 200 feet from home plate.

There are also differences for the various age groups. For boys and girls from 13 to 18, the pitcher is just 40 feet from home plate. For the nine to 12 year olds, the distance is 35 feet. In this age group, the bases are also shortened to 45 feet apart. Women's fast pitch competition also has the 40 foot distance from pitching rubber to home plate.

The pitching rubber is 24 inches across and six inches wide, while home plate is 17 inches across and 17 inches deep. The back half is diamond shaped. Batter's boxes are three feet wide and seven feet deep. The bases are all 15 inches square and can be no more than five inches thick.

The standard softball field is somewhat smaller than a baseball field. The bases are just 60 feet apart and the pitching rubber is 46 feet from home plate. In woman's softball, the rubber is 40 feet from the plate. For youngsters, the bases and pitching distance may even be shorter.

SOFTBALL FIELD

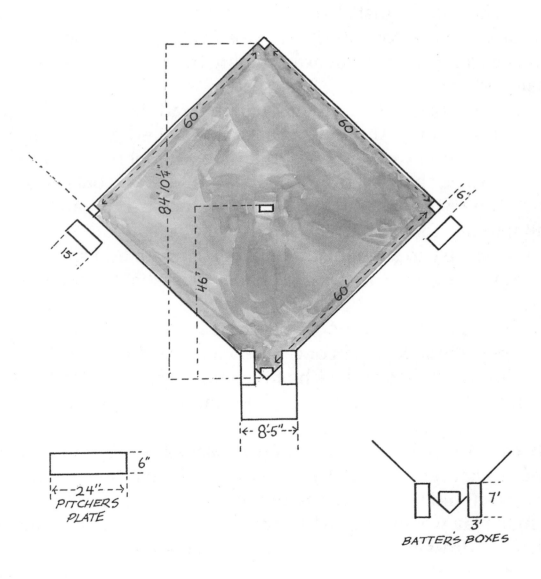

Years ago, the sport was called softball because the ball was actually very soft, often mushy. Today, a new softball is very hard, almost as hard as a baseball, but larger. A standard softball cannot be less than 11⅞ inches or more than 12⅛ inches in circumference (that is, the distance around the ball).

Softball bats are thinner and lighter than baseball bats. The bat can be no longer than 34 inches and cannot have a diameter of more than 2¼ inches at its thickest spot. Junior size bats begin at 26 inches long and go up in length an inch at a time to the largest, at 34 inches. Bats must also have a safety grip, made from cork, tape or an approved material. This safety grip cannot be less than 10 inches long and cannot extend more than 15 inches from the small end of the bat.

Today, of course, bats are made in the traditional wood or the newer aluminum. Aluminum bats will cost perhaps two or three time as much as wooden ones, but they will not break. Only the grip has to be changed from time to time. A wood bat can shatter at any time, so you should take care not to use a bat (any bat, really) to hit stones or anything other than a softball. A batter should also try to keep the trademark facing up and slightly to the rear when hitting. There is less chance of the bat breaking this way.

Softball players can choose between a glove and a mitt. However, only a first baseman or catcher can wear a mitt. A glove has a place for the thumb and each of the four fingers. The mitt has a separate place for the thumb and one large compartment for all the fingers.

Because a softball is larger than a baseball, softball gloves have deep pockets and tough webbing to trap the ball easily. All players should take good care of their gloves or mitts. Never allow them to stay wet or dirty. They should be treated with some kind of leather dressing every few weeks to keep the leather clean and

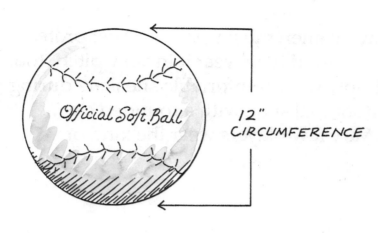

A regulation softball is 12 inches in circumference and has a tanned cowhide or horsehide cover. While not as hard as a baseball, today's softballs are nevertheless rather hard, especially when new.

soft and to prevent cracking. Needless to say, bats should also be kept clean, and wood bats especially should not be allowed to remain wet.

Catching equipment in softball is very basic. Catchers must wear a mask. The mask is well padded and light in weight. Because the ball is large, there are only a couple of bars protecting the face. Boys and men are not required to wear chest protectors,

Both wood and aluminum bats are used in softball. As a rule, the bats are lighter in weight and thinner than those used in baseball. It is up to each player to find the bat that is just right for him.

ALUMINIUM

WOOD

but girls must. In adult play, women must wear the chest protector in fast pitch, and it is suggested they wear it in slow pitch, too.

Many softball players simply wear comfortable sneakers during their games. Others wear a softball shoe with a rounded cleat made of rubber or plastic. Very few players wear the kind of

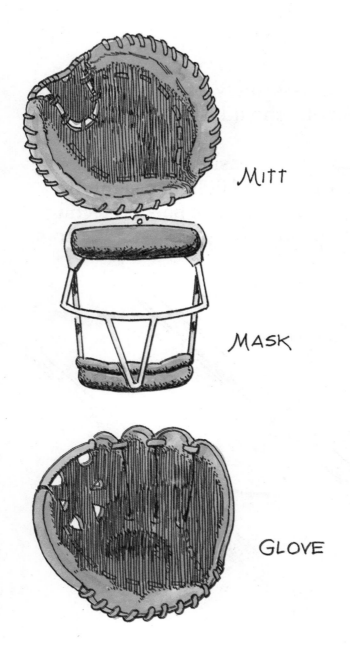

Mitt

MASK

GLOVE

Other softball equipment includes gloves, mitts, and a catcher's mask. Only the first baseman and catcher can use a mitt. Gloves must be used at all other positions. But both must be cared for and treated with a leather conditioner regularly. The mask is lighter in weight than those used in baseball. A helmet and throat protector must also be worn by all catchers through the high school level.

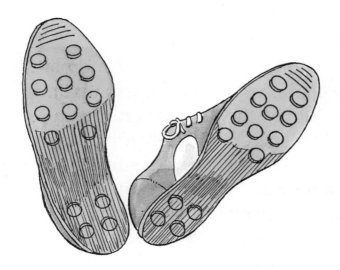

Many softball players simply wear sneakers when they are playing. Others choose to wear shoes with a circular, molded cleat, like those shown in the illustration. They give good traction and are far less dangerous than the metal cleats used in baseball. Yet a few softball players will sometimes wear metal cleats. There is no rule against them. But always check with your coach and see what your league allows.

metal-cleated shoes that are worn in baseball.

Uniforms are also very basic. Some teams simply wear T-shirts with the name of the ball club on it, jeans and a cap. Others may also have loose-fitting softball pants. Girls and women often wear shorts. There are really many different type uniforms that can be worn. In general, uniforms should be loose-fitting and comfortable. Tight, binding clothing will prevent a player from bending and stretching or simply be uncomfortable.

Batting helmets are required, but always check with your coach or league. Some leagues may require all players to wear helmets. It is also a good idea to wear helmets in the fast pitch game, where the ball can sometimes be thrown as fast as a baseball.

For reasons of safety, players cannot wear any kind of jewelry, such as watches, bracelets and especially neck chains while they're playing. If you have some jewelry on at game time, let a friend or family member hold it for you until the game is over.

Whether you are on a school team or just play in a weekend or evening league, you should always take pride in your appearance. Keep your equipment clean and in good condition. Always have a clean, dry uniform at the start of the game. Developing good habits from the beginning will help you become a better player.

Getting Ready To Play

As with any sport, it is not a good idea to just go out and play. Before every practice and every game, you should warm up and loosen your muscles. There may not be the kind of running in softball that there is in basketball or soccer, but there are many quick stops and starts. Even swinging the bat puts a sudden strain on muscles. If a player hasn't warmed up, he can easily pull a shoulder, back or rib cage muscle by just swinging.

Running the bases, fielding and chasing balls in the outfield all mean quick stops and starts. Without stretching and warming up, a player can get injured more easily. The same goes for your throwing arm. Throwing long or hard without warmimg up can lead to an injury.

Therefore, it is necessary for every player to warm up before practicing or playing. A good way to start is with some basic exercises. Push-ups and sit-ups will begin to get your body loose. Touching your toes with your knees straight or bent just slightly will loosen your leg muscles.

You can loosen the hamstring muscles in the back of your legs by putting one leg straight up in front of you on a rail or perhaps on the bleachers. Then lean forward at the waist and slide both hands along your outstretched leg, reaching for your ankles. This should be done slowly, perhaps five times with each leg. When you've reached as far as you can, hold that position for five or 10 seconds.

Another good leg exercise is to stretch one leg out to the side, keeping your knee straight. Then go down into a half squat on your opposite leg, which will stretch out the muscles of the first leg even more. Go down into the half squat slowly, then hold the position for five or 10 seconds. Repeat it with your other leg stretched out and the opposite leg squatting. As with all stretch-

A good warm-up routine should be followed before all practices and games. This stretching exercise loosens leg and thigh muscles. It should be done slowly, switching legs. As with all stretching exercises, hold the final position for about five to ten seconds. If there is any pain or discomfort, stop!

ing exercises, there should be no real pain or discomfort. If there is, then stop.

Still another leg, back and stomach exercise is to lie on your back and raise both legs slowly over your head until they touch the ground behind you. Hold the position a few seconds, then lower them before raising them once again. A similar exercise involves raising one leg at a time with the other leg still on the ground. Put both hands behind your thigh and pull on your leg until the muscles in your legs are stretched. As with the other ex-

Pulling up on each leg is another good warm-up exercise. It loosens leg and back muscles and helps get you ready to play.

ercises, hold the position and then do the same thing with the other leg.

Players can get ready to hit by stretching with a bat in their hands. Hold the bat at each end, then bring it straight over your head. From that position, bring your arms slowly to one side until the opposite shoulder and back stretch; then bring the bat over to your other side. Swinging a weighted bat around with each arm, then both, will also get you ready to hit. Finally, take a few hard cuts with your normal stance. These bat exercises can be done just before each turn at bat.

This is another warm-up exercise that looks something like a hurdler's stretch in track. The object here is to loosen the inside thigh muscles. Once again, alternate legs and feel the stretch as you lay back. Hold the position for five or so seconds. Then repeat with the other leg.

Your throwing arm should also be warmed up slowly. Before a game or practice, begin by playing catch with a teammate. Don't stand too far apart at the beginning. Just lob the ball back and forth. Be sure to throw with a full, easy motion. After a few minutes, you can begin to throw harder and at a greater distance. In about 10 minutes, your arm should be warm and ready.

It might also be a good idea to do some jogging before practice, maybe even a few wind sprints. After practice is also a good time to get in some extra conditioning. A few more exercises and some running will never hurt. The better shape a ball player is in, the better he will play. There is also less chance of getting hurt.

Getting ready to play softball or any sport also means taking care of yourself away from the ball field. Your body is like the rest of your equipment. It must be kept in tip top shape if you want to play your best. This means making sure you get enough sleep and eat the right foods.

It's all right to have a treat once in while, but a steady diet of junk food, fatty foods and sweets is not good. A balanced diet is important. Include plenty of fresh fruits and vegetables. Also drink plenty of fluids. Fruit juices and plain water are the best, especially on hot summer days when you perspire a lot.

It should go without saying for any athlete that alcohol and tobacco are bad. They will hurt your performance and maybe get you thrown off the team. The other rule to remember is to say no to drugs. There are no exceptions to this whatsoever!

Knowing how to train and getting ready to play are very important. Even a top player will not do his best if he doesn't have good everyday habits. He should warm up and exercise the right way before practice and games. No one is too good to get hurt, so it helps to do everything you can to stay fit.

LEARNING HOW TO PLAY

Learning How To Pitch

There is a great deal more skill involved in fast pitch softball than in slow pitch. Anyone who wants to try fast pitch must follow a number of rules and learn to pitch the right way. Then it takes a great deal of practice to really become good at it. By contrast, the slow pitch delivery is very simple.

In a sense, the motion for slow pitch is like the motion someone would use to roll a ball. However, the pitcher cannot swing the ball higher than his or her hip on either the backswing or the forward swing when the ball is released.

A right-handed pitcher begins with his right foot on the rubber, the toe or one spike just over the end. The left, or rear foot, is comfortably behind so that the pitcher feels balanced. The ball is held in both hands as the pitcher faces the batter. As in baseball, the catcher will give the pitcher a target with his mitt. The pitcher should never take his eye off the target until he has completed his delivery.

The pitcher begins the delivery by taking the ball in his pitching hand, then striding toward the batter with his rear foot. As he strides, he swings his pitching arm directly back, making sure not to raise the ball higher than hip level. He also shifts his weight from his foot on the pitching rubber to his front foot. Then he begins the forward swing of his arm.

In slow pitch, the most important thing is getting the ball over the plate. So each delivery should be identical. The pitcher starts with his pitching foot on the rubber, the opposite foot maybe eight or ten inches behind. As the pitcher swings his right arm back, he begins stepping or striding across the rubber with his left foot.

The ball should be released a split second after the striding leg has come down and as the pitcher completes the weight shift from back to front. This motion should be smooth and must become automatic. Because in slow pitch softball, a pitcher *must* be able to get the ball over the plate.

It has been said that a good slow pitch pitcher should be able to put seven or eight of 10 pitches into the strike zone. That's how important control is to pitching success. As mentioned, the pitcher must be able to throw each pitch exactly the same way.

One thing to remember is to open your hand as you release the ball. If you keep your hand cupped and allow the ball to roll off your fingertips, it will not roll off the same way each time. This can cause control problems. Another trick is to move around on the rubber a bit. If you keep throwing the ball to the right of the

As the arm swings forward, the striding leg is planted and the pitcher begins shifting his weight from the back to the front leg. Throughout the entire motion, the pitcher should keep his eyes fixed on the target provided by the catcher.

The release should come as the weight is completely shifted to the front foot. At that point, the heel of the rear foot comes off the pitching rubber. The pitcher should complete the motion with the smooth follow through. His back leg should be brought forward, even with the front leg and shoulder's width apart. His glove should be out in front of him so he is prepared to field his position if the ball should be hit back to him.

plate, move to the left a bit before you begin your delivery. You can be anywhere on the rubber as long as your foot is in contact with it.

If you are pitching too high or too low, you should change your stride. If the ball is coming in too high, a longer stride might help. If the ball is low, try to shorten your stride to bring the ball up.

It is not easy to throw a variety of different pitches in slow pitch. About the only different type of pitch possible is the change up. The change up can be gripped two ways. The first is a five-fingered grip. Most pitchers will throw their regular pitch with two or three fingers gripping the ball, depending on the size of the pitcher's hand.

Using a five-fingered grip, the pitcher will deliver the ball with the exact motion as his regular pitch. At the point of release, he will straighten his three middle fingers so that only his thumb and little finger are in contact with the ball as it leaves his hand. This release slows the ball as well as the spin.

The other way to throw the same pitch is to dig the fingernails of two or three fingers into the ball. This is similar to the way a knuckleball is held in baseball. If the pitcher flicks or snaps those fingers out as he releases the softball, the result is a change of pace.

As you might guess, the first way of holding the change is best for the beginner or for a pitcher with small hands. Either way, the pitch takes practice so that the pitcher can control it and perhaps throw the hitter off balance.

Remember, with slow pitch, consistency and control are the keys. The pitchers must throw each pitch the same way and get most of the pitches in the strike zone. A change of pace, or change up, every now and then will keep the hitters off balance. The fielders will have to do the rest.

Fast pitch is a different story. Now the total skill of a pitcher can affect the outcome of a game. The pitcher can throw as hard as possible. He can also throw a variety of curves, drops, rises and other pitches that take a great deal of practice to learn well. A great softball pitcher like Eddie Feigner or Joan Joyce can set down hitters the same way a Dwight Gooden or Roger Clemens can in baseball.

Of course, the first thing a new pitcher must learn is speed and control. It is one thing to throw fast. But if you cannot get the ball over the plate, all the speed in the world won't help. Once a fast pitch pitcher has speed and control, he must then add something else. He's got to be able to throw a number of different kinds of pitches. Good hitters will begin to hit even a great fastball if the pitcher doesn't mix it up with other pitches.

Three of the pitches that almost all good fast pitch pitchers use are the *rise*, the *drop* and the *change-up*. Others will also throw several kinds of curves, as well as a knuckleball. It takes time and a great deal of practice to master these different pitches.

Let's start with the two basic deliveries used mostly in the fast pitch game. They are the *slingshot* and the *windmill*. Both ways enable a pitcher to throw very hard. It's up to each hurler to decide which delivery is best for him.

Because there is less arm motion with the slingshot delivery, many feel young pitchers who use it will have better control. The pitcher begins in the same ready position as with the slow pitch delivery. As he strides forward with his back leg, he also begins the backswing with his arm. At the same time, he begins shifting his weight forward.

When his arm is fully extended upward, the pitcher cocks his wrist and turns his body slightly to the side of his pitching arm. As his striding foot comes down facing home plate, his arm is brought around in a strong, whipping motion. His back leg helps power the pitch by pushing off the rubber. The ball is then released with another snap of his wrist.

His arm comes up to complete the follow-through. At the same

The slingshot is perhaps the more popular of the two fast pitch deliveries. The pitcher begins as with slow pitch, with one foot on the rubber and the other slightly behind.

time, all the weight has been shifted to his front or striding foot. Then his back foot follows the motion off the mound and is brought up even with his front foot. The pitcher is now ready to field his position.

Most of the power in the pitch comes from a short, powerful stroke. A pitcher using the slingshot delivery must get in a groove so that his motion is exactly the same on every pitch. This is the only way to get good control when throwing hard. The arm swing and release, especially, cannot vary.

The same rules apply to the windmill delivery. But because the windmill requires a full, 360 degree swing of the arm, some pitchers have trouble controlling the softball. That's why the windmill can lead to wildness.

As she strides forward, she brings her pitching arm straight back and up behind her head, beginning to shift her weight forward as she goes. At the top of the backswing, her body is rotated away from the plate slightly and the wrist is cocked, so it will be ready to snap.

The arm is brought downward with a powerful, whipping motion. The ball is released with the snap of the wrist at the same time the weight shift to the front foot is completed. The pitcher then brings her rear foot even with the front foot to get ready to field her position.

29

Another fast pitch delivery is the windmill. Because the arm makes a complete, 360 degree circle, some people feel that pitches are harder to control using the windmill delivery. The starting position for the delivery is the same as for slow pitch and the slingshot. But this time as the pitcher begins his stride, he brings his arm forward. His palm is down as he starts the full circle swing.

A pitcher using the windmill starts the same way. He has both hands on the ball, his push-off foot on the rubber and his striding foot perhaps 12 inches behind. As he begins to stride, he also swings both arms forward. His pitching hand holds the ball toward the ground, palm down.

His gloved hand stops about waist high, but his pitching hand continues up and over his head, with his arm fully extended. The pitcher should use the full circle of his arm to build momentum. So the speed of his swinging arm should increase as it comes around the top of his head. As his arm begins to come downward, the pitcher completes his stride and shifts his weight from rear to front.

As with the slingshot, the speed of the arm generates power when it comes down. The ball should again be released with a

The arm is at the top of the swing as the stride is almost completed. When the pitcher starts the downward thrust, he also begins shifting his weight from the rear to the front leg. At this point, the rest of the motion will be almost identical to the slingshot.

The ball is released after a powerful thrust of the arm and snapping of the wrist. The rear leg is then brought forward as the pitcher completes his follow through. The windmill can produce a great deal of power and speed. But it is a delivery that takes a lot of practice for a young pitcher to master.

31

strong snap of the wrist just as the arm is straight down to the ground. As with the slingshot, the pitcher should follow through by completing the arc and bringing his rear foot off the rubber even with his front foot.

A young player who wants to try the fast pitch game should always begin with the slingshot delivery. It is easier to learn and much easier to control for someone just learning. Once he has good speed and control, he may want to experiment with the windmill. But many pitchers who begin with the slingshot seem to stick with it. Again, it's often a matter of control.

Speed and control are just the first steps for a fast pitch pitcher. Next come the different pitches that make a hard thrower a real pitcher. Most good fast pitch pitchers will throw a rise, a drop, a curve, a change-up and perhaps even a knuckleball to go with the occasional straight fastball.

The basic fastball is generally gripped with the first two fingers across the seam of the softball. The third and fourth fingers are off to the side of the ball, with the thumb gripping the seam opposite the first two fingers. At the delivery point, the thumb is on the top and the fingers underneath the ball. All three fingers are in contact with the ball at the point of release.

As in baseball, some pitchers' fastballs will have more movement than others. The good softball pitcher mixes pitches all the time and tries to keep the batter off balance. Many pitchers prefer to throw a ball that rises or drops, rather than one that comes in straight.

The *drop pitch* is held the same way as the fastball. The difference is in the release. Some pitchers just allow the ball to roll off their two fingers, giving it the rapid, downward spin that will cause it to drop. It might also help to pull your hand up at the point of release to give the ball even more of a downward spin.

Some pitchers will lift their thumbs off the ball a split second

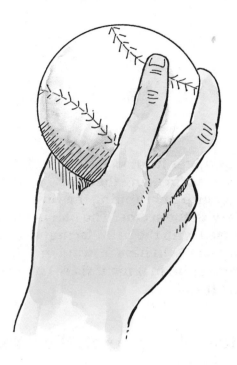

This is the basic fastball grip for the pitcher. The ball is held with the first two fingers across the seams and the thumb underneath. The third and fourth fingers are off to the side. In fact, the same grip is used for several pitches. Only the release is different.

before the release. Combined with the upward snap of their hands, they feel it helps with the downward spin and movement. Each pitcher will have to see which way works best for him. However, the drop is an important pitch that must be learned and mastered for fast pitch softball.

The trick to throwing the *rise* is to make the ball spin backward. Some pitchers use the fastball grip, only with their fingers running with the seams. As they swing their arms through the power part of their motion, they turn their hands over. Now their palms are downward, their fingers on top of the ball. When the ball rolls off their fingertips, it will have a rapid backward spin, causing the pitch to rise as it nears home plate.

A more difficult pitch to throw is the curve. Young pitchers should not throw curves too often because the twist of the wrist could put too much strain on their elbows. Some pitchers will throw a curve with a grip much like the fastball grip. However,

One grip for the rise has the pitcher again using the two-finger grip but running the fingers with the seams. The ball is released with the palm facing down so it will have upward or reverse spin, making it rise as it nears the plate.

the fingers are a bit closer together. At the release point, the wrist is rotated or snapped in a clockwise direction. This will give the ball the kind of spin that will cause it to curve.

The change of pace, or change-up, and the knuckleball were both discussed in the slow pitch section. The slow pitch change-up was thrown with a five-finger grip or a knuckleball grip, digging the fingernails into the ball. With fast pitch, most pitchers seem to prefer the knuckleball grip because now they will sometimes get the effect of both pitches.

In other words, the ball will float up to the plate much slower than any of the other pitches, even though it is thrown with the same motion. Because a knuckleball has little or no spin, the ball may also ''dance'' on the air currents, making it even harder to hit.

A good fast pitch pitcher must learn to mix his pitches and keep the hitters off balance. To do this, he needs several of the pitches described above. He must be able to get them over the plate and put them just where he wants them. He should also move his pitches around—up and down, inside and outside.

Being able to do these things and working closely with his catcher, the pitcher will find he is hard to beat.

Learning How To Hit

There are some differences between hitting a softball and hitting a baseball, but there are also some things that are the same. Perhaps the hitting rule most common to both games is simply to hit all you can. Practice hitting, and when you finish, practice some more. There is no substitute for swinging the bat against real live pitching.

At first glance, hitting a softball might sound easy. After all, the ball is bigger than a baseball, and the bats are lighter and thinner than baseball bats. However, this can cause a problem. If you are always trying to hit the ball as far as you can, chances are you won't hit well at all. If you don't hit a softball almost dead center, you're simply going to pop it up or hit it on the ground.

In softball, the best kind of hit is a line drive, a ball that goes past or just over the infield and maybe between the outfielders. Grounders can be scooped up by good infielders, and high lazy flies will be caught by sure-handed outfielders. Line drives will get the job done.

This is true of both the slow-pitch and fast-pitch games. In fact, with the ball floating toward home plate in slow pitch, there is always a strong desire to swing hard and try to kill the ball. In fast pitch, a hitter must go after the ball. There is no time to second guess. With the mound just 40 or 46 feet from home plate, the ball can really get there in a hurry. A hitter cannot afford to be too picky and wait for the pitch he wants. And he has to make a split second decision and attack the pitch. To wait on a ball may well mean missing it.

In slow pitch, the most important things are concentration and hitting technique. Concentration almost goes without saying. A hitter must concentrate on the ball and watch it from the moment it leaves the pitcher's hand. He must look at each turn at bat as a one-on-one battle that he will try to win by hitting safely.

The thing that will help him do this is good hitting technique and a smooth, level swing. Part of a good hitting technique is the ability to stride, shift weight and follow through with a fluid motion. Good hitting technique also means knowing the strike zone. In softball, the strike zone runs the width of home plate (17 inches) from the batter's armpits and the top of his knees. A hitter always has a better chance to hit a ball in the strike zone.

The choice between wood and aluminum bats is strictly up to each player. More and more teams are using aluminum bats because they don't break. No matter which kind you use, make

Every batter must know the strike zone. It is 17 inches wide from one side of the plate to the other. It also goes from the batter's armpits to the tops of his knees. A hitter must always be ready to swing at a pitch within this zone.

sure you feel comfortable with it. You should be able to swing it easily. If the bat is too heavy, you can't. So make sure the bat is the right one for you.

It's also important to have a comfortable batting stance. The stance is the way a player stands at home plate waiting for the pitch. No two players have exactly the same stance. As a rule, a young players should use a square stance, with both feet the same distance from home plate. Your feet should be spread at about shoulder width, with your knees slightly bent.

Your arms should be held away from your body, elbows out, with the bat at an angle just above your shoulder. By holding your arms and elbows this way, there is little chance of getting jammed or tied up by an inside pitch. It will also be easier to get the head of the bat out onto the ball with this method of hitting.

As the pitch is delivered, the batter will stride forward with his front foot. At the same time, he will extend his arms back, then pivot with his hips in the direction of the pitcher. The swing follows the pivot of his hips. First, his arms bring the bat through; then, his wrists snap the bat into the ball at the point of contact. He completes his swing by rolling his wrists over, and he follows through by bringing his bat past his front shoulder.

A strong, level swing can produce a number of different kinds of hits. For instance, if the batter meets the middle of the ball, he will hit a solid line drive. If he hits the ball just below the center, the ball will rise as it leaves the bat. The result is a fly ball or a pop up, depending on how far below center contact is made.

If the contact is above the center, the ball will go downward, producing a ground ball. Whether the ball is a hit or an out depends on where it goes. A good hitter will have some control over where the ball goes.

When the contact is made just as the ball is going past him, the batter will most likely hit it right back up the middle of the field. If

At the plate, a young batter must have a comfortable stance. A good way to start is with the feet about shoulder width apart and even in the batter's box. The knees should be bent slightly, with the bat held off the back shoulder and the elbows away from the body. If the elbows are too close to the body, the batter can easy be tied up, especially on an inside pitch. Once in the box and ready, the hitter must never take her eyes off the pitcher.

As the pitcher delivers, the hitter strides forward with her front foot. At the same time, she brings her arms back, extending her front arm at the elbow. All the while, she should follow the flight of the ball with her eyes.

At the point of contact with the ball, the hitter snaps her wrists for extra power, then rolls the top wrist over to begin the follow through. The heel of the rear foot is now off the ground because the weight shift has been completed. The hitter must also keep her head down until contact has been made. The follow through should be complete, with the bat coming around in a natural arc. Never cut a swing short.

The swing begins with the batter pivoting at the hips and beginning to shift her weight from her back foot to her front foot. The hips come around first, followed by the movement of the arms and the bat. The swing should be smooth and level, with the object to make contact right in the middle of the ball.

he swings just a bit sooner and makes contact when the ball is still in front of his body, he will "pull" the ball. For a left-handed hitter, the ball will go toward right field. The right-handed hitter will pull the ball toward left field.

By contrast, if the hitter swings a bit late, when the ball is already passing him, then he will hit it to the opposite field. The left-handed hitter will hit it to left and the right-handed hitter to right. There are times when a hitter will want to pull the ball and times when he may want to hit to the opposite field. If he is good enough, he can do it. But the beginner should always try to meet the center of the ball and hit it straight back through the middle of the diamond.

Different types of hitters will grip the bat in different ways. Bigger, stronger hitters will usually hold the bat right down at the end, above the knob. These are the hitters with home run power, and they often take a harder swing than other players. This doesn't mean they shouldn't follow the basic techniques of hitting. By taking a harder swing, they can hit the ball farther with more of a chance of a home run or an extra base hit. But they also may miss the ball more often.

A smaller player who doesn't have the power will sometimes "choke up" on the bat. This means gripping it a few inches above the knob or end. A choke hitter normally doesn't swing as hard as a power hitter, but he often has more bat control. In other words, there is a better chance of the choke hitter putting the bat on the ball and not missing.

A new player might be better off choking up at first. That way, he can work on just meeting the ball. Then, with the help of his coach, he can decide what kind of a hitter he wants to be. He might find himself better off gripping the bat a few inches from the end. Then, as he grows bigger and stronger, he can slowly change.

In the fast pitch game, a good pitcher with a lot of speed and "stuff" can be very difficult to hit. Because the pitching rubber is relatively close, pitches such as the drop and rise sometimes break very late. In fact, they almost break at the same time they reach the plate. One trick is to take a long stride and lunge a bit for the ball.

This doesn't mean to fall forward or lunge out of control. It simply means to get the bat out quicky and try to make contact with the ball a split second before it reaches the plate. That way, you can sometimes catch it before it rises or drops. If you can do that, you will be hitting a regular fastball. It takes practice to do this well, but it is one way to hit a pitcher with very good stuff.

In softball, especially the fast pitch game, there are not a lot of home runs. In fact, some people have described softball as a game of singles and doubles. So learn how to hit well, meet the ball, and get those line drives. If you can do that, you will be a valuable hitter for your team.

If you play slow pitch softball only, there is no need to bunt. Bunting is not part of the slow pitch game. In fast pitch, bunting can be as vital as it is in baseball and every player should learn how to bunt. It may look easy, but if you don't practice how to do it, you simply won't be successful at it.

There are two ways to bunt. In the first way, the batter will square around. This means he slides his top hand halfway up the bat and turns to face the pitcher. He will hold the bat loosely in his hands, making sure to keep his top hand behind the bat so that his fingers cannot be hit by the pitch. The bunter won't really swing at the pitch. Rather, he will let the ball hit his bat and bounce off. This way, the ball will not roll very far from home plate.

The batter will try to direct the ball. Sometimes he will try to push the ball toward first base. Other times he might try to bunt

All players should know how to bunt. The basic form has the batter "squaring" around to face the pitcher as the ball heads for the plate. He then slides his top hand at least halfway up the bat, making sure his fingers are protected behind the bat, not out in front where they can be hit by the ball. The bat should be kept level and should be held with a very loose grip. This will allow the hitter to control the bunt and make sure it doesn't come off the bat too hard and go directly to a fielder. Bunting is not as easy as it looks and should be practiced very often.

toward third. Whichever way he bunts, he is trying to keep the ball away from the infielders. This style of bunting is often used to move a runner up a base. It's called a *sacrifice bunt* because the batter is often thrown out at first, sacrificing his turn at bat. If the base runner moves from first to second, or second to third safely, then the batter has made a good bunt.

This style of bunting can also be used on the "squeeze play" when the batter bunts in an attempt to allow a runner on third base to score. With a *safety squeeze,* the runner waits to see where the ball is bunted. He then must decide whether he can make it home safely or not. With the *suicide squeeze,* the runner breaks for home as soon as the ball leaves the pitcher's hand. All the batter has to do is bunt the ball in fair territory and the runner will usually score.

The batter does not always have to square around to bunt well. If he is bunting for a base hit, he can shorten up on the bat and drop the bunt down as he begins running toward first base. A good bunter who can handle the bat can also bunt in any direction while using this method.

A player who can really bunt well can help his team in a number of ways. It's just another part of hitting that every player must learn and then practice.

Hitting, of course, is an important part of softball. In slow pitch, it's sometimes more difficult than it looks. In fast pitch, it appears difficult and it is. It's important for beginners to learn the right technique. This means getting a comfortable stance and working on a level swing. Then they must try to contact the middle of the ball, hitting it right back through the middle. If a player can do that, chances are he will soon become a very good hitter.

Learning To Play The Field

No matter how good a pitcher might be, he always needs solid support from his teammates in the field to win. In other words, defense will play a big part in the final result of a ball game. In slow pitch, the ball is almost always hit by the batter. Because of this, there is a tenth defensive player on the field. He's usually used as a short fielder, playing behind the infielders but in front of the outfielders. Fast pitch, in which there are more strikeouts, uses a standard nine-player defense in the field.

Sure hands and accurate throws are as important in softball as they are in baseball. In fact, speed and quickness, especially in the infield, might be even more important in softball because the bases are a shorter distance apart in softball (60 feets versus 90 feet) and the fielders have very little margin for error. Just the slightest bobble of a ground ball in softball and the batter will be safe.

Because of this, a fielder must know what to do with the ball the second he gets it. There is no time to think about where to throw or the game situation. That must be done ahead of time, before the play begins. In most cases, all throws should be made overhand. That is the best way to make a straight, hard throw. A fielder should throw sidearm or underhand only when there is no other choice.

Now let's look at each of the individual fielding positions.

The Catcher

It's not easy to be a catcher. In fact, good catchers are always in demand. If you think you might want to be a catcher, give it a try. If you get good at it, you'll always have a place to play.

A catcher has to be in very good shape because he has to squat down and get back up more than a hundred times in each game. He must also be smart. The catcher is almost like a coach on the field. He must know exactly what is happening in the game at all times.

To begin with, the catcher must "call" the game for the pitcher. He does that by signaling for the kind of pitch he wants. This is done before each pitch. The catcher places his right hand on the inside of his thigh and flashes the signals with his fingers. One finger can be a fastball, two a rise, three a drop and four a change-up.

Most catchers will give their signals while in a full squat or crouch. Just before the pitch is delivered, they will rise up slightly. That way, they can move quickly for a pitch that is off target, or they can get a quick throw away when a runner tries to steal. They will also be able to pounce out in front of the plate to field a bunt or a topper. Coming out of the full squat before a pitch is especially important when there are runners on base.

This is the basic catching position. The catcher is giving the pitcher a good target with his mitt. He is keeping his non-catching hand behind his leg to avoid getting hit by foul tips. It takes practice and a large mitt to become a good one-handed catcher. And there are many other things to learn about the position, as well.

The catcher must also be able to throw with a quick, snapping motion. The throw should be made from a point just behind his right ear, his forearm and wrist used to snap the ball off. That way, the throw will travel low and on a line. On high pop-ups, either behind or directly in front of the plate, the catcher should not flip his mask away until he has found the ball. Then he should throw it in the opposite direction, well away from him, so there is no chance of tripping over it and missing the ball. The catcher should get right under the ball as quickly as possible to easily handle any drift of the ball as it comes down. Most catches should be made with the glove facing up and held above the head.

On tag plays at the plate, the catcher should wait for the throw in front of the plate on the third base side. This gives his fielders a target. When he gets the ball he should grip it tightly in his bare hand and then protect that hand with his mitt. It's not necessary to block the plate unless the play is going to be extremely close. Otherwise he should get the ball down and let the base runner slide into it.

45

Among the many things a catcher must do is to remind his fielders of the game situation. This means telling them how many are out and where to throw the ball in certain instances. He must also try to know the hitters so he can call the right pitches. As we said earlier, catching is not easy.

First Baseman

The first baseman must be able to field his position very well. He will be taking throws from his infielders all game long. He has to catch the ball whether it's high or low, to the right or left, or even in the dirt. And he must do this with one foot on the bag to complete the out at first. All this takes a great deal of practice.

Besides being outstanding with the glove, the first baseman should be very agile. That's because he must be able to shift his feet around the bag very quickly as he moves for the throws. As a rule, the first baseman wears a large mitt instead of a glove. This helps when reaching for and scooping throws. It takes practice and skill to handle the mitt well.

On a ground ball to one of the other infielders, the first baseman should run quickly to the bag and stand squarely in front of it. He must then be ready to move in the direction of the throw. If the throw is coming on the home plate side of the bag, a right-handed first baseman would put his right foot on the corner of the bag. He would then stretch out with his left leg and his left hand to make the catch. A left-handed first baseman would put his left foot on the bag and stretch with his right leg and right hand to catch the same throw.

For throws on the outfield side of the base, the footwork is reversed. A right-hander puts his left foot on the bag and stretches out with his right leg. A lefty does it the other way. All first sackers must really practice their footwork. They can only do this

A first baseman must be as quick with his feet as he is with his glove. When he moves to the bag to take a throw, he has to judge quickly where the throw will be and then shift his feet. In this illustration, the ball has come in to the left of the bag, so the first baseman puts his right foot on the corner of the bag and ''stretches'' for the throw with his left leg. If the throw had been to the right of the bag, the first baseman would have had to touch the bag with his left foot and stretch with his right leg. The footwork for a lefthanded first baseman is just the opposite.

by taking many, many throws from their infielders. Footwork must become second nature to them.

On grounders hit right at them, first basemen must follow the same rules that apply to other infielders. They should get down low, bending at the knees, and put their gloves right down to the ground so the ball won't go under them.

As a first baseman, you will have to work very closely with both the pitcher and catcher on bunts and pop-ups. If you are going to catch a pop-up, make sure you call it loud and clear. And if you're going to field a bunt or slow grounder, call it so that someone else can cover the bag.

In some ways it's easier for a lefty to play first because he can make throws to any other base without shifting his feet. However, many righties have also become very good first basemen because they were willing to work hard and practice.

Second Baseman

The second baseman must be a very quick player. He's got to be able to move to both his right and left. He must also cover second base on steal attempts and cover first when the first baseman fields a bunt. He has to be able to make the difficult pivot to complete a double play.

In most instances, the second baseman plays between first and second. Exactly where he plays depends on the hitter. As a rule, the second baseman has a shorter throw than the shortstop or third baseman, so he doesn't normally need as strong a throwing arm. However, he has to put some mustard on the ball when making the double play.

Fielding ground balls is a big part of playing second. Like the other infielders, the second baseman begins each play in the ready position. This means feet spread apart, knees bent, glove down and close to the ground. As the pitch is made, the second sacker rocks up onto the balls of his feet, ready to move quickly in any direction.

Ground balls should always be taken low and close to the ground. The second baseman, like other infielders, should come up throwing, beginning to step toward first as soon as the ball is in the glove. Thus, when he straightens up, he has already started his throwing motion and can get the ball away quickly. A quick throw is always very important in softball.

Slow grounders should always be charged with short, quick steps. When you reach the ball, be sure to get down low when fielding it. Don't back up on hard hit balls, either. To let the ball play you that way can often lead to an error.

This is the ready position for all infielders. They should get into this stance before every pitch. The feet are spread comfortably apart, glove open and held low. The fielder should bend at the waist and watch the hitter. As the pitch is thrown, the fielder will rock up on the balls of her feet and be ready to move quickly in either direction.

On tag plays, the second sacker should position himself directly in front of the bag, feet spread apart. He has to be ready to move in either direction for a bad throw. If the throw is on target, he will be in position to just let the base runner slide into his glove for the out. If the throw is high, he has to bring the ball down fast to try to make the tag.

On pop-ups over his head, a second baseman can either back-pedal or run back sideways. Either way, he must be sure to keep his eye on the ball and always call for a ball he can catch. Calling for the ball avoids collisions on the field.

Perhaps the toughest play for the second baseman is the double play. With a runner on first and less than two outs, there is the possibility of a DP any time the ball is hit on the ground. If the ball is hit to the second baseman, he must time his throw to the shortstop, who will be cutting across the bag. The throw should reach the bag just as the shortstop is coming across. That way, he can make the putout and relay the ball to first for the twin killing.

If the ball is hit to short or third, the second sacker must make

Working together is an important part of all softball teams. Here the shortstop has flipped the ball to the second baseman, who is set to relay it to first for a doubleplay. Infielders must practice the doubleplay every day. Timing is all important. The shortstop must make the throw at just the right moment to give the second baseman room to pivot and throw. When done right, it is an exciting play.

the pivot. When the ball is hit, he runs quickly to the bag. He must catch the throw from short or third with his foot on the bag, then turn his body and fire to first. There will be times when the base runner tries to take him out with a hard slide. The second baseman must avoid the runner while making his throw at the same time. Sometimes he has to do this while leaping high in the air.

They say that practice makes perfect, and for the second baseman, learning the skills takes practice.

The Shortstop

In many ways, the shortstop provides the glue that holds the infield together. He must cover a lot of ground quickly, to both his left and his right. In addition, he must have a very strong throwing arm, be able to catch pop flies and also turn the double play.

On plays up the middle, the shortstop will often have to throw while off balance. When he makes a play deep in the hole to his right, he has the longest throw of any infielder. That's why a shortstop in softball needs that strong throwing arm.

Like the others infielders, the shortstop gets down in the ready position before each pitch. On balls hit to his left or right, he should begin moving with a crossover step. If the ball is hit to his left, he will pivot on his left foot and cross his right foot in front of his body to start after the ball. When he moves to his right, it is his left foot that crosses over. This method assures the shortstop of a quick start.

Throws should be made overhand and on a straight line. Whenever possible, the shortstop should set himself before throwing. If he has to go to his right deep into the hole, he should plant his right foot before making the overhand throw. For a ball

All infielders, especially the shortstop and second baseman, will sometimes have to cover a lot of ground in a hurry to reach a ground ball. The best way to start after a ball is with a big crossover step. This is done by springing out of the ready position and swinging one leg across your body in the direction of the ball. A hard push from your back leg should give you good momentum. After the crossover step to get started, you should go the rest of the way with short, quick strides.

hit right at him, he should be moving toward first as he picks it up, striding with his left foot. This way he already has momentum when he makes his throw.

On slow-hit balls that he must charge, the shortstop can throw sidearm because of the speed in getting the throw away. He must also be ready to tag runners at second, using the same rules that apply to second basemen. He must always be ready to go after any pop fly on his side of the infield. In fact, it is sometimes easier for a shortstop to catch a pop-up behind third because he has a better angle on the ball than the third baseman.

The shortstop doesn't really have to pivot on the double play. However, he must cross the bag at the same time he takes the throw from the second baseman and then make a strong throw to first while avoiding the runner. On balls hit up the middle, he may also step on second himself, then fire to first for the DP.

A shortstop can be a busy man during the course of a game. He has to make many different kinds of plays, and to do that well, he must work very hard. His team depends on him.

Third Baseman

In baseball, third base is called the hot corner because so many hard-hit balls come that way. With softball, the same nickname can apply. A third baseman has to be ready for some very hard-hit balls. He often has to jump and dive for them. He must also be ready to charge in for bunts and slow rollers and to catch pop flies. Along with everything else, he must have a very strong throwing arm.

Quickness, rather than speed, is important for the third baseman. He must have the kind of reflexes that allow him to move very quickly to his right or left. He also has to have a very quick and sure glove. On hard-hit balls, a third baseman doesn't get a second chance.

This is the correct way to field a ground ball. The infielder should be low to the ground and have his glove right at ground level. If he brings the glove up too soon, the ball might go right under it. As he scoops the ball up, the infielder should begin striding toward first and make his throw in a quick, smooth motion.

Though most throws from third will be made overhand, the third baseman will sometimes have to pick up a bunt barehanded. When he does this, he will usually throw sidearm just to get the ball away quickly. On plays in which he has to dive, he may have to throw from his knees or even from a sitting position. A strong arm helps here.

Knowing the hitters also helps. When a pull hitter is up, the third baseman plays closer to the line. If a light hitter who likes to bunt is up, the third baseman will come in closer to home plate. Like the other infielders, he always starts in the ready position.

All four infielders must also be prepared to take cutoff throws from the outfielders. If a ball is hit to a deep part of the outfield, one of the infielders will run halfway out to take a relay throw. In other words, he cuts the ball off on its way in and whirls to make a stronger throw to the base, usually home or third. Cutoff men are needed when the outfielder is so far out he cannot make a strong throw to the base by himself.

There are some special things that each infielder must learn about his position, and there are some other things that all the infielders must learn. Some players can play more than one infield position. They are called "utility" infielders. Others play the one position they like best. If someone does that, he should try to become the best player he can.

The Outfield

In fast pitch softball (as in baseball), there are three outfielders—the left fielder, center fielder and right fielder. Slow pitch has the same three, plus an extra man, usually a short fielder. He is almost a combination of infielder and outfielder. We will deal with him separately.

All outfielders should have good speed, though the centerfielder is usually the fastest because he has the most ground to cover. Outfielders should all have strong throwing arms.

An outfielder must have good instincts for the ball. He must be able to sense where a ball will be hit and get a good jump as soon as the ball leaves the bat. Some of this is natural ability. Some can be learned by practicing and studying hitters. Besides catching fly balls and line drives, an outfielder must also be able to charge base hits and pick them up much like an infielder. A ball getting through an outfielder's legs could be a disaster.

Outfielders should always try to catch the ball two handed. A one-hand catch may look cool, but there is too great a chance to drop the ball. It's best to catch a fly ball with your glove just above your shoulder. Keep your bare hand just to the outside of the glove, and then cover the glove with that hand once the ball is in.

If you have to run a long way for a ball, then you may have to try for a one-hand catch. Also remember to call all fly balls between yourself and another outfielder. You've got to work with the outfielder nearest you to avoid possible collisions.

Throws should always be made overhand and on a straight

No fly ball can be taken for granted. Even with a routine, lazy fly, an outfielder must be careful. He should get directly under the ball, spread his feet for balance and catch with ball over his head with *two hands*! A one-hand catch may look cool, but for young people just beginning to play, it can be a bad mistake.

line. A high, floating throw takes too long to reach its target. With runners on base, outfielders should always field the ball ready to throw. On a high fly, for instance, they should position themselves a step or two behind the ball. Then, just before making the catch, they should step up so they are already moving forward and can step right into their throw.

The same is true when fielding a bouncer. Charge the ball and take it as you're stepping into the throw, just like an infielder, so

Long throws from the outfield should always be made with an overhand motion. While the outfielder must get the ball away quickly, he must still set himself. As he begins to throw, he should shift his weight from back foot to front. The ball should be delivered overhand, with the shoulder leading. Then the arm snaps the throw back toward the infield. A good, strong throw will be on a straight line, not lofted high in the air. Besides throwing hard, it is also important to be accurate. A wild throw is a poor throw, no matter how far it travels.

there is no time wasted. Outfielders must also back each other up. If the left fielder is moving into left center to cut off a base hit, the center fielder should run over behind him. This way, if the ball should get through, the backup man will be there.

All outfielders must know how to play the hitters. If a right-handed pull hitter is up, the entire outfield will swing around to left. If the batter is one who hits in all directions, then the outfield will play straight away. Outfielders should take a ready stance similar to the infielders. They don't have to put their gloves down real low, but they should be ready to move in either direction very quickly.

Outfielders cannot go to sleep if a lot of action isn't coming their way. They must always know the game situation and always know where they are going to throw the ball on each play. They should also learn about each ballpark. If the outfield has a fence, the outfielders should know their distance from it so they won't have a collision.

The short fielder is only used in the slow pitch game. Playing in an area just behind the infield, he must combine the skills of both an infielder and an outfielder, picking up ground balls and throwing like an infielder. On hard-hit balls, he may even throw out a runner at first or second, so he must have a strong throwing arm.

He also has to catch short flies, pops and line drives over the infield. Because he is in the middle of the diamond, he must talk to both infielders and outfielders. He sometimes has to direct traffic like a policeman, because it can get crowded out there.

Because he doesn't have a set position, the short fielder can

Outfielders must learn to back each other up. When one outfielder goes to field a rolling or bouncing base hit, the outfielder closest to him should always run behind to back him up. If the ball should get past the first outfielder, the back-up man might save an extra base or two, or even a run.

play the hitters more freely than the other fielders. This can be a big advantage if the coach or the short fielder himself knows the hitters well. There are even times when the short fielder can become a fourth outfielder. There is no doubt that this tenth man can really help a defense, especially in a game in which almost every hitter puts the ball in play.

Every defensive position on a team is important. A crisp fielding team can do as much to win ball games as a strong hitting team. A good team will practice fielding as much or more than hitting. As is the case in other sports, the team making the fewest mistakes will usually win.

Learning To Run The Bases

A good base runner does not always have to be fast. Of course, speed helps, but a player who knows the game can make up for a lack of speed with smart base running and good sliding. A bad base runner can easily make mistakes, and mistakes always hurt a team.

To watch a smooth base runner is to watch someone circle the bases without breaking stride. He will cut each bag easily, running slightly wide before rounding the base. He knows just how to step on the inside corner of each bag and then push off toward the next, making a smooth, but crisp turn that won't cause him to lose any speed.

When running to first on a ground ball, run as hard as you can and straight through the base. First is the only base you are allowed to overrun. But stay alert. The throw may be wild, and if it is, you can go on to second. Of course, if you get a hit, you make the turn at first so you're ready to go on to second if the ball is misplayed.

Any time you're running to third with thoughts of going home, make sure to watch the third base coach. He will signal you to either stop or to keep running. He will also let you know whether to slide or come into the base standing up. When a runner is coming home, it's the job of the next hitter to signal a slide or a stand-up score.

A quick start is very important to a base runner. It can mean the difference between being safe or out. Or it can result in an extra base or being safe on a steal attempt. Even when leaving the batter's box, the quick start is an advantage. The secret to the quick start is short, powerful steps that will get a runner up to full speed quickly. The runner should use long strides once he has reached full speed.

There will also be times when every base runner has to slide. Sliding is a skill that takes a lot of practice. If you slide wrong, you can easily sprain an ankle, or worse. The simplest slide is the

The first slide all young players should learn is the straight-in, or pop-up slide. It is the easiest to learn. With this slide, the impact is taken by the leg and hip. Hands should be held off the ground, fists slightly clenched to avoid jammed fingers. One leg is bent underneath the other, and this is what allows the runner to pop right up. As he hits the bag with his front leg, he pushes upward with the other leg and his momentum will bring him right back to his feet. After a player learns this slide, he can begin working on other types, such as the hook slide and fallaway.

straight in, or *pop-up*, slide. The runner comes into the base at full speed. He starts to slide by putting one leg out straight and folds the other under it. When his front foot hits the bag, he will use his other leg to push himself right back to a standing position.

One variation is to slide straight in without folding one leg underneath. This way, the runner won't pop up. The advantage of the pop-up slide is that the runner will be all set to take another base should the throw be wild.

A tougher slide to master is the *hook slide*. Using this method, the runner will slide to one side of the base or the other. As he does, he will hook the base with his trailing leg. He can hook the base with his leg bent under him, or he can fall further away and hook it with his leg bent outward. Some call this version of the slide the *fall away*. Either way, it's a tough slide on the body, but it can be very effective.

Some runners use a *headfirst slide*. It involves diving for the bag while running full speed, but there is a greater risk of injury. It's

There is no stealing in slow pitch softball. In fast pitch, however, there is stealing, but no leading until the ball is pitched. This is the position the baserunner should assume when getting ready to run. He will stride over the bag with his right leg, then push off the bag with his left. The trick of good baserunning and stealing is to reach full speed as quickly as possible. This is done by taking short, powerful steps for the first 10 or 15 yards. As you do this, slowly straighten up and lengthen your stride.

also a slide that can lead to scratches, scrapes, bumps and bruises all over the body. It's up to each player (with help from his coach) to decide how he wants to slide.

Base stealing isn't as big a part of softball as it is in baseball. In fact, there is no stealing allowed in the slow pitch game. In fast pitch, runners can steal, but they can't take a lead. They can only leave the base once the ball has left the pitcher's hand.

To get ready to run in fast pitch, the base runner stands facing the next base. He has his left foot on the base, his right foot just behind it. As the ball leaves the pitcher's hand, the base runner swings his back foot forward and pushes off the bag with his left foot. The first few steps should be strong and short, the runner pumping his arms hard and bending forward like a sprinter. The faster he reaches full speed, the better his chance of stealing the base.

Because there is no leading in softball, the faster runners are usually the best base stealers. Stealing is a weapon and can help a team to win, as can good, all-around base running.

The sport of softball is a fun game, a mainly amateur game and a game meant for everyone. Some players prefer fast pitch, others slow pitch. Some play both. It's a game that can be played for basic Sunday exercise, or it can be played at the league level. The fast pitch game is the more skilled version. It can be as competitive as baseball, and some of the players are outstanding.

Fast or slow, softball is very popular and still growing. If you feel you want to play, give it a try, but be sure to learn something about the game. It helps to have a coach to assist you with the fundamentals. The better you get, the more you will enjoy the game, and softball is a game you can really enjoy, especially when you play well.

Softball is fun for boys and girls, young and old alike. It can be played for a weekend of fun, or in a regular league several times a week. No matter how often you play, there is still a big thrill when you have performed well for the fans and your team-mates.

GLOSSARY

Arc ball   A fairly new form of softball pitch in which the ball is pitched slowly and with a very high arc.

Bases   Three square canvas bags placed 60-feet apart. With home plate, they form the shape of a diamond.

Batter's box   A chalked-lined rectangular area, three feet wide by seven feet long, drawn on each side of home plate. The batter must stand inside this box.

Bunt   An intentional short hit, usually in the area of home plate. It is used to advance a runner, score a runner from third, or as an attempt for a base hit. Bunting is not allowed in slow pitch, only fast pitch.

Calling the game   A phrase that refers to signals given to the pitcher by the catcher, telling him what kind of pitch to throw and where to throw it.

Change up   Type of pitch that looks like a fastball, but comes in a lot slower. It is used to throw hitters off balance.

Choke hitter   A hitter who grips the bat several inches up from the knob end.

Control   The ability of a pitcher to throw strikes and to put the ball just where he wants it.

Cutoff man   The middle man on a long throw, usually from the outfield. The cutoff man moves into position to take the throw and then relays it to the appropriate base.

Delivery   Term used to describe the way a pitcher throws the ball to home plate.

Double   A safe hit by which the runner winds up on second base.

Double play   Fielding play that results in two players on the hitting team being called out.

Drop   A pitch that drops sharply as it approaches home plate. It is delivered with a forward spin on the ball.

Fast pitch   A style of softball in which the pitcher is allowed to throw the ball as fast as he can.

Force-out   A play in which a runner must try to advance to the next base, but is called out when the fielder with the ball touches the base first.

Home plate   The base where the batter stands when he hits. The plate is 17 inches across, square in the front, and diamond-shaped in the back. It is usually a flat piece of hard rubber.

Home run   A fair hit in which the batter circles all the bases. It can either pass over the outfield fence or roll far enough away from the outfielders to allow the hitter to score.

Hook slide   A slide in which the runner goes past the base and hooks it with his trailing foot.

Hot corner A term used to describe third base because so many hard-hit balls come in that direction.

Knuckleball A type of pitch that doesn't spin and often moves or "dances" with the air currents.

Line drive A hard-hit ball that travels on a straight line several feet off the ground.

Pitching rubber A rectangular piece of hard rubber or wood that the pitcher's foot must contact during his delivery.

Pivot Term used to describe the action of the second baseman when he takes a throw from the shortstop, touches second base, then throws to first to try for a double play.

Pull hitter A hitter who usually hits the ball down the line in the direction of his swing. A righthanded hitter will pull the ball to left field, and a left-handed hitter will pull to right.

Rise A type of pitch that moves upward suddenly as it approaches home plate. It is thrown with a reverse or upward spin.

Sacrifice A short hit, usually a bunt, in which the batter tries to advance the runner, even though the batter may be thrown out.

Short fielder An extra or tenth player used in slow pitch who usually plays in front of the centerfielder.

Single A safe hit by which the batter winds up on first base.

Slingshot A type of fast pitch delivery in which the pitcher brings his arm straight back, then powers the ball toward the plate.

Slow pitch The style of softball in which the pitcher can throw only at moderate speed. This makes control all the more vital.

Squeeze play An exciting play in which the batter bunts the ball in an attempt to allow a runner on third to score. With the safety squeeze, the runner waits to see where the ball is bunted. But with the suicide squeeze, the runner breaks from third as soon as he legally can.

Stance The way the batter stands at home plate ready to hit.

Steal A play in which a baserunner advances one base on a pitch that the batter takes. Stealing is only allowed in fast pitch, not slow pitch.

Straight-in slide A slide in which the runner heads straight for the base with no deception.

Tag play A play in which a fielder tries to tag the runner with the ball before the runner reaches the base.

Triple A safe hit in which the batter winds up on third base.

Umpires The officials who run the game. The umpires call balls and strikes, judge balls to be fair or foul, and make the out and safe calls at the bases. There are usually between two and four umpires at a softball game, depending on the league.

Utility fielder Name given to a fielder who can play several positions, usually in the infield.

Windmill Type of pitching delivery in which the pitcher makes a complete counterclockwise circle with his arm before delivering the ball to the plate.